Everyday Prayers

FOR CHILDREN

Everyday Prayers

FOR CHILDREN

ideals children's books™

Nashville, Tennessee

ISBN 0-8249-5475-0

Published by Ideals Children's Books
An imprint of Ideals Publications
A division of Guideposts
535 Metroplex Drive, Suite 250
Nashville, Tennessee 37211
www.idealsbooks.com

Color separations by Precision Color Graphics, Franklin, Wisconsin

Printed and bound in Italy

Library of Congress CIP data on file

For Ann Alise

Designed by Jenny Eber Hancock

10   9   8   7   6   5   4   3   2

ACKNOWLEDGMENTS

FARJEON, ELEANOR. A prayer from *Prayer for Little Things*, Houghton Mifflin, 1945.
Copyright by Eleanor Farjeon. Reprinted by permission of Harold Ober Associates
Incorporated. Our sincere thanks to those authors we were unable to locate.

O God, this little prayer I pray:
Please take good care of things—
Of all the little things that walk
Or fly with tiny wings.

For we are in this great big world
And sometimes are afraid,
So please take care of all the things,
O God, that you have made.
Amen.

—George L. Ehrman

Before I rise to meet the day,
I fold my hands and softly say:
Dear Lord, may everything I do
Bring me closer unto you.
Amen.

—Rosaleen Schmutz

Thank you, God, for all your gifts;
Thank you for your graces.
Thank you for your loving care
About us in all places.
Amen.

—Rosaleen Schmutz

We thank thee, Father up in Heaven,
For all the blessings thou hast given:
For home and friends and daily food
And everything that is so good.

We thank thee for the work and play
As we go to school each day,
For Jesus' love and Jesus' care
That travel with us everywhere.

Help us to be both kind and true,
To do the things we ought to do.
Keep us free from sin and blame,
And save us all in Jesus' name.
Amen.

—Edwin Osgood Grover

For honeysuckle's fragrance rare;
For new-mown hay that sweetens air;
For katydids that sing at night
And lightning bugs with taillights bright;

For open fires and crackling wood;
For Mom's hot cocoa, steaming good;
For sunshine dancing on a rug;
For buttermilk from Grandma's jug;

For meadows green and shady creeks
Where Mr. Frog in gusto speaks;
For old church bells that sweetly ring—
I thank thee for each little thing!
Amen.

—Laurie Wilcox

Dear Lord, as I kneel down to pray,
Help me to know thy will today.
Help me to be serene and still
And rise to do thy holy will.

Guide all my thoughts and deeds today;
Guide every step along the way.
And when the day at last is through,
Let me be thankful, Lord, to you.
Amen.

—Elizabeth Ann M. Moore

We thank thee, Lord,
For birds and flowers,
For trees and winds
And gentle showers.

We thank thee
For our clothes and food,
For friends and parents,
Kind and good.

And, Lord, we thank thee
For our play,
And sleep, when tired
At close of day.
Amen.

—Herbert Stoneley

Lord, make my life a little light
Within the world to glow;
A little flame that burns so bright,
Wherever I may go.

Lord, make my life a little hymn
Of tenderness and praise;
Of faith that ne'er grows dim,
To all your wondrous ways.
Amen.

—M. Betham-Edwards

I thank thee, Lord, for all thy lovely things:
For singing birds, for trees and flowers of spring,
For purple mountains wearing crowns of snow
That look across green valleys far below.
I thank thee for thy presence, ever near,
And constant care that keeps us from all fear.
Amen.

—Rhea Hendricks

For flowers that bloom about our feet,
Father, we thank thee;
For tender grass so fresh and sweet,
Father, we thank thee;
For the songs of birds and hum of bee,
For all things fair we hear or see,
Father in Heaven, we thank thee.

For this new morning with its light,

Father, we thank thee;
For rest and shelter of the night,
Father, we thank thee;
For health and food, for love and friends,
For everything thy goodness sends,
Father in Heaven, we thank thee.
Amen.

—Ralph Waldo Emerson

God made the sun
And God made the tree;
God made the mountains
And God made me.
I thank you, O God,
For the sun and the tree,
For making the mountains,
And for making me.
Amen.

—Leah Gale

Teach me, my God and King,
In all things thee to see,
And what I do in anything,
To do it as for thee.
Amen.

—George Herbert

Thou art great and thou art good
And we thank thee for our food.
Amen.

—Author Unknown

Lord, make us glad each day
For all the fun along our way;
For work and games and sun and showers,
And wind and rain to grow our flowers.

For houses along the busy street;
For family and friends we greet;
For everything we do and see
Is good—because it comes from thee.
Amen.

—Author Unknown

Heavenly Father, hear my prayer:
Keep me in thy loving care.

Guide me through each lovely day
In my work and in my play.

Keep me pure and sweet and true
In everything I say and do.
Amen.

—Abbie Burr

Lord, teach a little child to pray,
And oh, accept my prayer;
Thou can hear all the words I say,
For thou art everywhere.

A little sparrow cannot fall
Unnoticed, Lord, by thee;
And though I am so young and small,
Thou can take care of me.
Amen.

—Author Unknown

Father, hear my prayer this morning;
Guide my footsteps through this day.
Around my heart with love adorning
Wrap thy peace so it will stay.

Give me of thy richest blessing;
Bathe me in thy golden light.
Let me feel thy strong hand pressing
Should I need it through the night.
Amen.

—Clarice Albritton

Day by day,
Dear Lord of thee
Three things I pray:
To see thee more clearly,
To love thee more dearly,
To follow thee more nearly,
Day by day.
Amen.

—Richard of Chichester

Dear Father, hear and bless
Thy beasts and singing birds.
And guard with tenderness
Small things that have no words.
Amen.

—Author Unknown

Loving Jesus, meek and mild,
Look upon a little child!
Make me gentle as thou art;
Come and live within my heart.

Take my childish hand in thine;
Guide these little feet of mine.

So shall all my happy days
Sing their pleasant song of praise;
And the world shall always see
Christ, the holy Child, in me.
Amen.

—Charles Wesley

Now I lay me down to sleep,
I pray thee, Lord, my soul to keep;
Thy love be with me through the night
And wake me with the morning light.
Amen.

—Author Unknown

Father, we thank thee for the night,
And for the pleasant morning light,

For rest and food and loving care,
And all that makes the day so fair.

Help us to do the things we should,
To be to others kind and good,

In all we do, in all we say,
To grow more loving every day.
Amen.

—Author Unknown

Now I wake and see the light,
Thy love was with me through the night;

To thee I speak again and pray
That thou wilt lead me all the day.

I ask not for myself alone,
But for thy children, everyone.
Amen.

—Author Unknown

Please, God, take care of little things—
The fledglings that have not their wings,
Till they are big enough to fly
And stretch their wings across the sky.

And please take care of little seeds,
So small among the forest weeds,
Till they have grown as tall as trees
With leafy boughs, take care of these.

And please take care of drops of rain,
Like beads upon a broken chain,
Till in some river in the sun
The many silver drops are one.

Take care of small new lambs that bleat,
Small foals that totter on their feet,
And all small creatures ever known,
Till they are strong to stand alone.

And please take care of children who
Kneel down at night to pray to you;
Oh, please keep safe the little prayer
That, like the big ones, asks your care.
Amen.

—Eleanor Farjeon

Come, Lord Jesus, be our guest;
Let this food to us be blessed.
Our hands we fold;
Our heads we bow;
For food and drink
We thank thee now.
Amen.

—Author Unknown

God is great
And God is good;
Let us thank him
For this food.
By his hands
We are fed;
Give us, Lord,
Our daily bread.
Amen.

—Author Unknown

God bless all those
that I love;
God bless all those
that love me;
God bless all those
that love
those that I love,
And all those that
love those
that love me.
Amen.

—Author Unknown